THE VOYAGE OF
SAINT BRENDAN:

Journey to the Promised Land

NAVIGATIO SANCTI BRENDANI ABBATIS
translated with an introduction by
JOHN J. O'MEARA

THE DOLMEN PRESS
North America: Humanities Press Inc.

Set in Pilgrim type with Hammer Uncial display
Printed in the Republic of Ireland by O'Brien Promotions Ltd.
for
The Dolmen Press
Mountrath, Portlaoise, Ireland
in association with
Humanities Press Inc.
171 First Avenue, Atlantic Highlands
New Jersey 07716, U.S.A.

First published in limited edition 1976
First trade edition 1978
Paperback edition 1981. Reprinted 1982, 1985.

Library of Congress Cataloguing in Publication Data

Brendan, Saint, Legend. English.
The voyage of Saint Brendan, journey to the promised land = the
Navigatio sancti Brendani abbatis.
Includes bibliographical references.
1. Brendan, Saint 484?–577?—Legends. I. O'Meara, John Joseph.
II. Title.
PA8295. B7E5 1976 398'. 23 76-13917

ISBN 0 85105 384 x *pb*

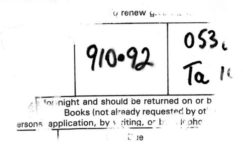
DOLMEN TEXTS I

Odiliae Peregrinanti

Heureux qui, comme Ulysse, a fait un beau voyage.
Joachim du Bellay

CONTENTS

The woodcuts in this book are reproduced from Sankt Brandans Seefahrt, *printed by Anton Sorg at Augsburg in 1476 and are here slightly reduced in size.*

INTRODUCTION

SAINT BRENDAN was born in Ireland some-time around A.D. 489, probably in or near Tralee in Co. Kerry. His name is connected with the foundation of a number of monastic settlements in the counties of Kerry, Clare and Galway and on islands in the river Shannon. One of the most famous of these monasteries was Clonfert in East Galway, where the story of the *Voyage of Saint Brendan* appears to begin. Brendan is reported as having visited Iona, the Orkney and Shetland Islands, Britain and Brittany. He died sometime between 570 and 583.

Brendan lived at a period when Irish monks were leaving their country in significant numbers to be on pilgrimage for Christ's sake and to spread the Gospel. Columba left Ireland for Iona in 563. Columbanus set out for France — to found a string of monasteries from Luxeuil to Bobbio — about 590. It was but the beginning of the hey-day of such pilgrimages. By 891 the Anglo-Saxon Chronicle reports that 'three Scots came to King Alfred in a boat without any oars from Ireland whence they stole away, because they would be in a state of pilgrimage for the love of God, they recked not where.' Many of these pilgrimages centred on the islands to the west, north and north-east of Ireland.

In due time Brendan became known as *the* voyager who sailed to and fro across the ocean, no longer in search of lonely islands in which to find solitude, but of the ever famous and ever elusive Promised Land.[1] Professor Carney has suggested that within a hundred years of his death there already existed a primitive account in Latin of Brendan's quest for that happy land. This account was ecclesiastical in general character, but influenced the creation of the secular, heroic *Voyage of Bran*, written in Irish, which goes back to the late 600's or early 700's. The Latin *Voyage of Saint Brendan*,[2] which is here translated, was written in Ireland perhaps as early as 800. Shortly afterwards this in turn influenced the creation of another secular, heroic voyage, the *Voyage of Mael Dúin*. These works form part only of a whole series of voyages or *Immrama*, some in Irish and some in Latin.[3]

1 Cf. G. Boas, *Essays on Primitivism and Related Ideas in the Middle Ages*, Baltimore 1948, pp. 154-174.

2 *Navigatio Sancti Brendani Abbatis*, ed. Carl Selmer, University of Notre Dame Press 1959. Selmer suggests (p. xxvii, n.12) that the author was Israel Episcopus. This conflicts with Carney's views.

3 J. Carney, *Medium Aevum* 32 (1963), pp. 37-44. H. P. A. Oskamp, *The Voyage of Máel Dúin*, Groningen 1970, thinks that the *Voyage of Saint Brendan* and the *Voyage of Mael Dúin* had a common source rather than that the latter was influenced by the former. One cannot enter here into the many complicated problems of all the *Immrama* — the relations of the oral with the written, the secular with the ecclesiastical, the pre-Viking with the post-Viking, the *Lives* with the *Voyages*, and so on. There is as yet no generally received opinion on these matters. Scholars should consult Carney's and Oskamp's works for bibliography in the first instance.

These *Voyages* were, of course, not uninfluenced by literary tales of other nations—by, for example, the renowned stories of the *Odyssey* and the *Aeneid*.[4] Nevertheless, even the most secular of them (such as the *Voyage of Mael Dúin*) shows a distinct Christian colouring, and one as ecclesiastical as the *Voyage of Saint Brendan* can rightly be called a Christian allegory. Renan has characterized it as 'sans contredit le produit le plus singulier de cette combinaison du naturalisme celtique avec le spiritualisme chrétien.'[5] Be that as it may, it is certain that it is predominantly monastic in outlook, and inculcates the doctrines and practices of the ascetic life as understood in an Irish environment.

This monasticism is a firm basis of reality in the story of Brendan's voyage. However distant the island visited, if there is human life there, its inhabitants follow the monastic life as known to the author. The story in other words clearly reflects such sea-journeys and visits to islands and island monasteries as Brendan himself is reported to have made. Some of these pilgrimages may well have reached Iceland, for the Irish are reported to have got there by around 795.[6]

This raises the question, of interest to many, if Brendan was the first to discover America? In 1580, for example, when John Dee entered in his

4 Selmer, *op. cit.*, pp. xxi, xxiv.
5 'La poésie des races Celtiques,' in *Essais de Morale et de Critique*, Paris 1913.
6 Dicuil, *de mensura orbis terrae*, VII, ii.

map a defence of England's title to North America, he mentioned Saint Brendan's voyage as a main part of the evidence.

Some recent books have suggested that Brendan did.[7] Ashe gives reasons for considering that the Irish got to Greenland by 900 at latest, and to the Sargasso Sea, well west of the Azores, about the same time. He suggests the identification, among other possibilities, of the Island of Sheep and the Paradise of Birds of the *Voyage of Saint Brendan* with the Faroes; the Island of Smiths with Iceland; the Island of Paul the Hermit with Rockall; the region of whales with Greenland; the region of fog with Newfoundland; the Island of the Community of Ailbe with Madeira; the Coagulated Sea with Sargasso; the Island of the Three Choirs with the Bahamas; and the Island of Grapes with, possibly, Jamaica. Even the rather sceptical Thomson,[8] writing in a context having nothing to do with Brendan's voyage, allows that it is most plausible that Iceland was reached even as early as about 320 B.C. by Pytheas of Marseilles. Likewise he does not, while being sceptical, dismiss the evidence that the Phoen-

---

7   e.g. Geoffrey Ashe, *Land to the West*, London 1962 (which will supply the reader with an initial bibliography to the question). Paul H. Chapman, *The Man Who Led Columbus to America*, Atlanta 1973. S. E. Morison, *The European Discovery of America*, New York 1971, pp. 1-31 is a better guide.
8   J. O. Thomson, *History of Ancient Geography*, Cambridge 1948, pp. 77, 150.

icians reached perhaps as far west as the Sargasso Sea in ancient times. The Romans certainly penetrated to the sea north of Scotland and may, like Pytheas, have also got to Iceland.[9] The authors who concern themselves with this question bring forward a great deal of evidence, of every level of value and none, from ancient and medieval times.

From some of this matter — from, possibly, the earlier *Voyage* suggested by Carney — and from the reports handed down of Brendan's voyages and the voyages of others, the author of the *Voyage of Saint Brendan*, who was clearly a bookish person, even if he had an ear sensitive to a folk-tale, could have drawn. If his hero, Brendan, did not get to America, others might have or at least could have got much of the way. Since Heyerdahl one knows that, given certain conditions, a small boat *can* make the crossing. To the contemporaries of the author of the *Voyage of Saint Brendan* the exploit can hardly have seemed more impossible than for our fathers a landing on the moon. But the *Voyage of Saint Brendan* hardly proves that he discovered America.

9 cf. Horace, e.g., *Odes* III, 3.54 ff. *uisere gestiens/qua parte debacchentur ignes/qua nebulae pluuiique rores.* The structure of this and similar poems in Horace points to a northern, rather than any other, location. Volcanoes, mists and rain are just the thing for Iceland and its approaches. Similarly *te beluosus qui remotis/ obstrepit Oceanus Britannis* (*ibid.* IV, 14.47f.) must refer to the monsters of the seas to be encountered in the Atlantic north of the British Isles.

Nevertheless, the tradition of Brendan's having not only voyaged, but discovered some western, fortunate, but lost island became in due course very persistent. The Island or Islands of Brendan feature on many a map, chart and globe between the thirteenth and sixteenth centuries and beyond. Their location is variously indicated all the way from Iceland to East of Newfoundland, to East of the Antilles, to West of the Canaries or the Azores.[10]

One can easily understand, then, that the *Voyage of Saint Brendan*, from being a tale told to delight and edify, became one of the most famous and enduring stories of western Christendom. Burghers, seafarers, cartographers and others were eager to discover what it had to say and how this should be interpreted. The story was especially popular in the Low Countries and Germany, where not only vernacular translations,[11] but new versions began to appear. It was natural that the Scandinavians and Normans should have a special interest in it: indeed the most famous version of the story was done in Norman-French early in the twelfth century. It is hardly surprising either that Ireland, Britain and Brittany were interested also. The Iberian countries

10   Cf. R. V. Tooley, C. Bricker, G. Roe Crone, *A History of Cartography*, London 1969, pp. 66, 71, 192, 204, 216; Raymond H. Ramsay, *No Longer on the Map*, New York 1972, pp. 82-85.
11   Carl Selmer, 'The Vernacular Translations of the *Navigatio Sancti Brendani* : A Bibliographical Study,' *Mediaeval Studies* 18 (1956), pp. 145-157.

were fascinated by the Island of Saint Brendan which they claimed as their possession. Venice and Genoa were equally under its spell. Some read a famous passage in Dante's *Inferno*[12] as referring not only to Ulysses, but to Brendan also.

*

The *Voyage of Saint Brendan*, nevertheless, merits attention above all in its own right. It has the direct and simple appeal of the description of the public life of Jesus and his disciples as found in the New Testament. The journeyings, miraculous meals, fears and wonders that happened around the Sea of Galilee are transferred to the Atlantic and a strongly insular context. When danger threatens their boat the disciples scurry for protection. The Master affords instant assurance: 'Do not be afraid!' Here lies the main inspiration of the work.

Immediately deriving from this is its monastic character — the chanting of the divine office, the prolonged fasts, the simple faith in and obedience to the Abbot, the monks' father. The institutions and practices of monastic life in an Irish environment are faithfully reproduced. These, along with the background of inter-island journeyings by the Irish monks, and precision in whatever references or implications there are to the topography of Ireland itself, supply a strong underpinning of reality to the tale as a whole.

12 xxvi, 100-142 : *ma misi me per l'alto mare aperto/
sol con un legno e con quella compagna/picciola. . . .*

At the same time it is most obvious, as Carney says, that it is a strongly integrated tale deriving, he would claim, from several centuries of literary tradition. It is not merely that it reproduces folk-motifs like the significance of some ultimate river such as Lethe or the motif of holding conversation with birds,[13] or echoes of episodes, such as that of Palinurus, from such literary epics as the *Aeneid*—it has also a remarkable and conscious employment of some literary devices. Epic repetition and symmetry are carefully cultivated. Similar episodes are described in similar and echoing phrases: the short account of the Promised Land of the Saints at the beginning is but expanded at the end; the brothers spend the same feasts on the same islands doing the same things; the sides of the meshes in the net around the Crystal Pillar are of equal length,[14] as are the sides of the pillar itself; the Island of Paul the Hermit is perfectly round and it is as long as it is wide as it is high; each of the fish at the bottom of the Clear Sea is a circle with his head touching his tail (an exploit, the author playfully adds, which Jasconius would emulate, but cannot, because of his length); the sheep on an island, the birds on a tree, and the fish circling the boat on one occasion are so dense in number that nothing of the island, or tree, or sea beyond the fish can be seen; all the trees on a

---

13 cf. F. Cumont, *After Life in Roman Paganism*, Yale 1923, p. 157; M. Eliade, *Daedalus*, Spring 1959, p. 258.
14 That is 6 to 7 feet — from which the maximum size of the boat can be roughly assessed : cf. p. 51.

certain island are of the same kind, are laden with the same fruit which will feed a monk (observing a strict fast, of course) for a ritual number of days. Journeys and fasts are repeatedly of forty days, or twenty, or fifteen, or three or two: the completion of the significant number seems to take precedence, when approaching an island, over tide or wind. There is also the employment of simpler rhetorical devices — the fondness for the tricolon, a run of three balancing phrases within the same sentence, for example.

All of this indicates how stylized, how abstract, how non-naturalistic (*pace* Renan) the narrative is. There is indeed the underlying reality of monastic life and the sense of space on the ocean — but one does not feel the salt spray or the plunging of the boat in heavy seas; one does not see the scudding clouds or wilt under the pitiless sun; one does not marvel at the reddening dawn, or the following moon, or the immensity of the stars in the heavens at night. It may take forty days to reach an island, but the reader does not feel them pass. There may be reality, but there is also suspension of reality.

The apogee of this abstraction is suddenly revealed in a flash in Chapter 12. Brendan asks: 'How can an incorporeal light burn corporeally in a corporeal creature?' This is precisely the kind of question which the ninth-century Irish philosopher, Eriugena, puts in his *de divisione naturae*.[15] It is

15 e.g. V.11 f. (*P.L.* 882C-883C), which also considers the question of light in this connection.

redolent of the schools. Yet it *is* only a flash. The
answer given comes from the Bible, not Eriugena.
The level of discreet and charming allegory is for
the most part carefully maintained. The story is one
indeed of miracles and monsters, of angel-birds and
blacksmith demons; but when it is placed side by
side with the *Voyage of Mael Dúin*, to which it is
certainly related, its simple sophistication — not
without humour — quickly emerges. It reminds one
reader at least of a Book of Hours in its conscious
and delicate *naiveté*.

*

The present translation into English is done from
the only scientific edition of the original Latin
text.[16] An attempt has been made to catch some of
the spirit of the original which, naturally, has many
of the characteristics of late weakened Latin : pro-
nouns, for example, are imprecise; *coepit* has become almost an auxiliary verb; *praedictus* usually
signifies little more than the definite article, and
quidam little more than the indefinite. Weakening

16 See n.2. For all its excellence, it has been criticized by
     Carney (*loc. cit.*) and L. Bieler, *Zeitschrift für Kirchen-
     geschichte* 1 (1961), pp. 164-169. One might add to
     these criticisms that Selmer's listing of Scriptural
     sources is neither complete nor accurate. Selmer's
     edition has already been translated into English by
     J. F. Webb in *Lives of the Saints*, Penguin 1965 : apart
     from its being now hard to discover, Webb's trans-
     lation falls short in a number of ways of what is
     desirable. The present translator follows Carney in his

of syntax is occasionally of staggering proportions. Scholars have seen the intrusion from time to time of Irish idiom. The translator has made silent judgment and exercised deliberate choices in handling these matters.

His one care has been accuracy and, as far as possible, precision. The number of scholars who nowadays have sufficient competence in Latin to use it scientifically is small and growing smaller. Yet, the number of students of the medieval period continually grows. Conscious of the way in which these depend on sometimes grossly inaccurate translations, one must strive both to report fully and not to mislead.[17] This is hard to achieve.

The importance of accuracy in translating a text such as the *Voyage of Saint Brendan*, which exercises such a fascination on historical researchers of

criticisms of the first few paragraphs of Selmer's text. He does not, however, accept that the *insula deliciosa* (mentioned twice in chapter 1) is different from the *insula deliciarum* in chapter 28 : the correspondence of the accounts of the visits to the Promised Land of the Saints strongly suggests that the same island was intended. While it would be agreeable to identify this island with Fair Island (said to be near the very impressive Slieve League in Co. Donegal) as the gateway, so to speak, of Paradise, one is not confident (among other considerations) that the Latin 'deliciosa' corresponds to the Irish 'Caín'.

17 'Most translations (of the *Voyage of Saint Brendan*) are souped up and utterly unreliable,' — Morison, *op. cit.*, p. 28. This remark applies to the one used by himself too.

various kinds, goes without saying. Nevertheless only Webb's translation, for example, correctly reports the original Latin text where it says (Chapter 28) that Brendan sailed *east* for forty days to the Promised Land of the Saints. This, moreover, accords with the situation of that land as given in Chapter 1. For the Promised Land of the Saints is, so to speak, next door to Ireland. Most writers follow other translators and send Brendan travelling for forty days west. Other obscurities have survived in earlier translations — mostly arising from an insufficient attention to indications of time, or failure to appreciate that time in a wonder story can be suspended, and in many ways.[18]

The translator must be very careful also not to be more precise than the text or the state of available knowledge allows. Brendan's boat is called *navis* and sometimes *navicula*: while the terms may have significance in comparisons, no other significance can be attached here to the difference in terminology. Similarly *navigare* is used in the text to mean 'travel by boat,' 'sail,' and 'row'; unless one specific meaning is *clearly* indicated one should refrain from using the more specific — for it may seem to afford evidence of detailed importance. To translate *vela* as 'sails' in such a phrase as *tendere vela*, when Chapter 4 specifically states that the boat was furnished with one sail, is to show a lack of knowledge of Latin idiom and send the

18   cf. Oskamp, *op. cit.*, pp. 59, 157.

reader on a false trail. And to translate *scaltis albis et purpureis* in Chapter 17 as 'white and pink grapefruit' is to wrest the evidence towards the identification of a particular location. On the other hand to translate *capsa* in Chapter 12 by 'reliquary' rather than, for example, 'vestment' is to follow the authority of a text of the eighth-ninth century. There are many such problems in this text.

Finally the translator has elected to use modern terms, when they indicate the same thing, instead of obsolete or specialized terminology. Thus he has used 'Easter' instead of 'Pasch', but kept 'Maundy' Thursday, because the washing of the feet is a greater reality in the story than it now is for us. He has substituted 'nine o'clock' for 'the third hour' and converted 'cubits' into 'feet' and so on — all to make the text as easily intelligible to an English reader in the twentieth century as a Latin in the ninth. He has supplied Contents and chapter headings to induce the reader to follow, and tell him where he has arrived.

But above all the translator has felt the need of illustrations. It has always seemed to readers that the *Voyage of Saint Brendan* demanded instantly to be made visual. Some of the most successful were woodcuts done in Augsburg by Anton Sorg in 1476, of which a number are reproduced here. Since, however, they relate to a late and embellished version of the *Voyage*, the reader must not expect them to correspond in detail with our text.

THE VOYAGE OF SAINT BRENDAN:
JOURNEY TO THE PROMISED LAND

NAVIGATIO
SANCTI BRENDANI
ABBATIS

BARRIND'S STORY

1 SAINT BRENDAN, son of Findlug, descendant
   of Alte, was born among the Eoganacht of
Loch Léin in the land of the men of Munster. He
was a man of great abstinence, famous for his
mighty works and father of nearly three thousand
monks.

When he was fighting the good fight, in a place
called Clonfert of Brendan, there arrived one evening one of the fathers whose name was Barrind, a
descendant of Niall.

When this Barrind was plied with many questions
by the holy father, he wept, prostrated himself on
the ground and stayed a long time praying. But

Saint Brendan lifted him up from the ground and embraced him, saying:

'Father, why should we be sad during your visit? Did you not come to encourage us? Rather should you give joy to the brothers. Show us the word of God and nourish our souls with the varied wonders that you saw in the ocean.'

When Saint Brendan had finished his remarks, Saint Barrind began to describe a certain island, saying:

'My son Mernóc, steward of Christ's poor, left me and sought to live the life of a solitary. He found an island near Slieve League, called the Delightful Island. Then, a long time afterwards I heard that he had many monks with him, and that God had shown many wonders through him. So, I set out to visit my son. At the end of a three-day journey, as I was approaching, he hurried with his brothers to meet me. For the Lord revealed to him that I was coming. As we were crossing in a boat to the island the brothers came, like bees swarming, from their various cells to meet us. Their housing was indeed scattered but they lived together as one in faith, hope and charity. They ate together and they all joined together for the divine office. They are given nothing to eat but fruit, nuts, roots and other greens. But after compline each remained in his own cell until the cocks crowed or the bell was struck. Having stayed overnight and walked round the whole island, I was brought by my son to the sea shore facing west, where there was a boat. He said to me:

3

"Father, embark in the boat and let us sail westwards to the island which is called the Promised Land of the Saints which God will give to those who come after us at the end of time."

'We embarked and sailed, but a fog so thick covered us that we could scarcely see the poop or the prow of the boat. But when we had spent about an hour like this a great light shone all around us, and there appeared to us a land wide, and full of grass and fruit. When the boat landed we disembarked and began to go and walk round that island. This we did for fifteen days — yet we could not find the end of it. We saw no plants that had not flowers, nor trees that had not fruit. The stones of that land are precious stones. Then on the fifteenth day we found a river flowing from east to west. As we pondered on all these things we were in doubt what we should do.

'We decided to cross the river, but we awaited advice from God. In the course of a discussion on these things, a man suddenly appeared in a great light before us, who immediately called us by our own names and saluted us, saying :

"Well done, good brothers. For the Lord has revealed to you the land, which he will give to his saints. The river there marks the middle of the island. You may not go beyond this point. So return to the place from which you departed."

'When he said this, I immediately questioned him where he came from and what was his name. He said :

4

"Why do you ask me where I come from or how I am called? Why do you not ask me about the island? As you see it now, so it has been from the beginning of the world. Do you feel the need of any food or drink or clothing? Yet for the equivalent of one year you have been on this island and have not tasted food or drink! You have never been over-come by sleep nor has night enveloped you! For here it is always day, without blinding darkness. Our Lord Jesus Christ is the light of this island."

'Straightaway we started on our journey, the man coming with us to the shore where our boat was. As we embarked in it he was taken from our eyes and we passed through the same darkness to the Delightful Island. When the brothers saw us they rejoiced with great joy at our arrival and com-plained of our absence for such a long time, saying:

"Why, fathers, have you left your sheep wander-ing in the wood without a shepherd? We knew of our abbot going away from us frequently some-where or other — but we do not know where — and staying there sometimes for a month, some-times for a fortnight or a week or more or less."

'When I heard this, I began to console them, saying to them:

"Think, brothers, only of good. You are living undoubtedly at the gate of Paradise. Near here is an island which is called the Promised Land of the Saints where night does not fall nor day end. Your abbot Mernóc goes there. An angel of the Lord guards it. Do you not perceive from the fragrance of our clothing that we have been in God's Paradise?"

'The brothers then replied:

"Abbot, we knew that you were in God's Paradise in the wide sea; but where that Paradise is, we do not know. We have indeed often noticed the fragrance exuding from our abbot's clothes when he returns from there after the space of forty days."

'I stayed on with my son for two successive weeks without food or drink. Yet our bodies were so satisfied that to others we seemed full of new wine. And after forty days I received the blessing of the brothers and the abbot and set off with my companions on the return journey to my cell. I shall go there tomorrow.'

When they heard these things, Saint Brendan and all his community prostrated themselves on the ground, glorifying God and saying:

'The Lord is just in all his ways and holy in all his works. For he has revealed to his servants such great wonders. He is blessed in his gifts, for he has nourished us today with such a spiritual foretaste.'

When they had said this, Saint Brendan spoke:

'Let us go to repair our bodies and to the washing of feet in accordance with the new commandment.'

When that night was over, Saint Barrind, having received the blessing of the brothers in the morning, set out for his own cell.

THE BROTHERS ASSEMBLE

SAINT BRENDAN, therefore, when fourteen brothers out of his whole community had been chosen, shut himself up in one oratory with them and spoke to them, saying:

'From you who are dear to me and share the good fight with me I look for advice and help, for my heart and all my thoughts are fixed on one determination. I have resolved in my heart if it is God's will — and only if it is — to go in search of the Promised Land of the Saints of which father Barrind spoke. How does this seem to you? What advice would you give?'

They, however, having learned of the holy father's will, say, as it were with one mouth:

'Abbot, your will is ours. Have we not left our parents behind? Have we not spurned our inheritance and given our bodies into your hands? So we are prepared to go along with you to death or life. Only one thing let us ask for, the will of God.'

VISIT TO SAINT ENDA

SAINT BRENDAN and his companions, therefore, decided to fast for forty days — but for no more than three days at a time — and then to set out. When the forty days were over he said good-bye to the brothers, commended all to the man put in charge of his monastery, who was afterwards his successor there, and set out westwards with fourteen brothers to the island of a holy father, named Enda. There he stayed three days and three nights.

THE BUILDING OF THE BOAT

4 **h**AVING RECEIVED the blessing of the holy father and of all the monks that were with him, he set out for a distant part of his native region where his parents were living. But he did not wish to see them. He pitched his tent at the edge of a mountain stretching far out into the ocean, in a place called Brendan's Seat, at a point where there was entry for one boat. Saint Brendan and those with him got iron tools and constructed a light boat ribbed with wood and with a wooden frame, as is usual in those parts. They covered it with ox-hides tanned with the bark of oak and smeared all the joints of the hides on the outside with fat. They carried into the boat hides for the makings of two other boats, supplies for forty days, fat for preparing hides to cover the boat and other things needed for human life. They also placed a mast in the middle of the boat and a sail and the other requirements for steering a boat. Then Saint Brendan ordered his brothers in the name of the Father, Son and Holy Spirit to enter the boat.

THE THREE LATECOMERS

WHILE SAINT BRENDAN remained *5* alone on the shore and blessed the landing-place, three brothers from his own monastery came up, following after him. They fell immediately at the feet of the holy father, saying:

'Father, leave us free to go with you wherever you are going; otherwise we shall die on this spot from hunger and thirst. For we have decided to be pilgrims for the days of our life that remain.'

When the man of God saw their trouble, he ordered them to enter the boat, saying:

'Your will be done, my sons.'

And he added:

'I know why you have come. One of you has done something meritorious, for God has prepared a suitable place for him. But for you others he will prepare a hideous judgment.'

THE UNINHABITED HOUSE

SAINT BRENDAN then embarked, the sail *6* was spread and they began to steer westwards into the summer solstice. They had a favourable wind and, apart from holding the sail, had no need to navigate.

After fifteen days the wind dropped. They set themselves to the oars until their strength failed. Saint Brendan quickly began to comfort and advise them, saying:

'Brothers, do not fear. God is our helper, sailor and helmsman, and he guides us. Ship all the oars and the rudder. Just leave the sail spread and God will do as he wishes with his servants and their ship.'

They always had their food, however, at evening time. When they got a wind, they did not know from what direction it came or in what direction the boat was going.

When forty days were up and all the victuals had been consumed, an island appeared to them towards the north, rocky and high. When they came near its shore they saw a high cliff like a wall and various streams flowing down from the top of the island into the sea. Nevertheless they failed totally to find a landing-place where they could put in the boat. The brothers were greatly harrassed by the lack of food and drink. So each took up a vessel to try to catch some of the fresh water. When Saint Brendan saw this, he said:

'Do not do that. What you are doing is foolish. God does not yet wish to show us a place to land, and do you want to be guilty of plundering? The Lord Jesus Christ after three days will show his servants a landing-place and a place to stay, so that our harrassed bodies will be restored.'

When, then, they had circled the island for three days, on the third day about three o'clock they found an opening where one boat might enter. Saint Brendan stood up immediately and blessed the entry. It was a cutting with rock of remarkable height on either side, straight up like a wall. When they had all disembarked and stood outside on land, Saint Brendan forbade them to take any equipment out of the boat. As they were walking along the cliffs of the sea, a dog ran across them on a path and came to the feet of Saint Brendan as dogs usually come to heel to their masters. Saint Brendan said to his brothers:

'Has not God sent us a good messenger? Follow him.'

Saint Brendan and his brothers followed the dog to a town.

On entering the town they caught sight of a great hall, furnished with beds and chairs, and water for washing their feet. When they had sat down Saint Brendan gave an order to his companions, saying:

'Beware, brothers, lest Satan lead you into temptation. For I can see him persuading one of the three brothers, who came from our monastery to follow after me, to commit a bad theft. Pray for his soul. For his body has been given into the power of Satan.'

The house where they were staying had hanging vessels of different kinds of metal fixed around its walls along with bridles and horns encased in silver.

Then Saint Brendan spoke to the one who usually placed bread before the brothers:

'Bring the meal that God has sent us.'

This man stood up immediately, found a table made ready and linen and a loaf for each of marvellous whiteness and fish. When all were brought before him, Saint Brendan blessed the meal and said to his brothers:

'Give praise to the God of heaven who gives food to all flesh.'

The brothers sat back, therefore, and glorified God. In the same way they found as much drink as they wanted. When supper was over and the office of compline said, he spoke:

'Rest now. There is a well-dressed bed for each of you. You need to rest, for your limbs are tired from too much toil.'

When the brothers had fallen asleep, Saint Brendan saw the devil at work, namely an Ethiopian child holding a bridle in his hand and making fun with the brother already mentioned to his face. Saint Brendan got up immediately and began to pray, thus spending the whole night until day. In the morning when the brothers had hurried to the divine office and later had gone to the boat, they saw a table laid out just like the day before. And so for three days and three nights God prepared a meal for his servants.

ONE LATECOMER DIES

7 AFTER THAT Saint Brendan with his companions set out again, saying to the brothers:

'Make sure that none of you takes anything belonging to this island with him.'

But they all replied:

'God forbid, father, that our journey should be desecrated by any theft.'

Then Saint Brendan said:

'Look, our brother whom I referred to a few days ago has a silver bridle in his bosom given to him last night by the devil.'

When the brother in question heard this, he threw the bridle out of his bosom and fell before the feet of the man of God, saying:

'I have sinned, father. Forgive me. Pray for my soul, that it may not perish.'

Immediately all prostrated themselves on the ground, praying the Lord for the brother's soul.

As they rose from the ground and the holy father

raised up the brother, they saw a small Ethiopian jump out of his bosom, wailing with a loud voice and saying:

'Why, man of God, do you expel me from my dwelling, where I have lived now for seven years, and make me depart from my inheritance?'

Saint Brendan replied to this voice:

'I order you in the name of the Lord Jesus Christ not to injure any man to the day of judgment.'

Turning again to the brother, the man of God said:

'Receive the body and blood of the Lord, for your soul will now leave your body. Here you will be buried. But your brother here, who came from our monastery with you, has his burial place in Hell.'

And so when the Eucharist had been received, the soul of the brother left his body, and before the eyes of the brothers was received by the angels of light. His body, however, was buried on the spot by the holy father.

A YOUTH BRINGS FOOD

8 *T*HE BROTHERS then went with Saint Brendan to the shore of the island where their boat was. As they were embarking a youth came up carrying a basket full of bread and a jar of water. He said to them:

'Receive a blessing from the hand of your servant. A long journey lies ahead of you until you find consolation. Nevertheless neither bread nor water will fail you from now until Easter.'

Having received the blessing they began to sail out into the ocean. They ate every second day. And so the boat was borne through various places of the ocean.

THE ISLAND OF SHEEP

ONE DAY they saw an island not far from them. When they began to steer towards it, a favourable wind came to their help, so that they did not have to exert themselves more than their strength could manage. When the boat stood to at the harbour, the man of God bade them all get out of the boat. He got out after them. When they began to go round the island they saw large streams of water, full of fish, flowing from various springs. Saint Brendan said to his brothers:

'Let us carry out the divine service here. Let us sacrifice the Spotless Victim to God, for today is Maundy Thursday.'

They stayed there until Holy Saturday.

Walking round the island they found various flocks of sheep — all of one colour, white. The sheep were so numerous that the ground could not be seen at all. Saint Brendan called his brothers together and said to them:

'Take what you need for the feast from the flock.'

The brothers, hurrying according to the command of the man of God to the flock, took one sheep from it. When they had tied it by the horns, it followed the brother who held the rope in his hand as if it were tame to the place where the man of God was standing. Again the man of God spoke to one of the brothers:

'Take a spotless lamb from the flock.'

The brother hurried and did as he had been enjoined.

On Good Friday, while they were preparing for the service, a man appeared to them holding in his hand a basket full of bread, that had been baked under the ashes, and the other things that were necessary. When he placed these before the man of God, he fell prone on his face three times at the feet of the holy father, saying:

'How have I deserved, O pearl of God, that you should eat, on these holy days, of the labour of my hands?'

Saint Brendan lifted him up from the ground, embraced him and said:

'Son, our Lord Jesus Christ chooses a place for us where we can celebrate his holy Resurrection.'

The man replied:

'Father, here you will celebrate Holy Saturday. Tomorrow, however, God has ordained that you celebrate the Masses and the vigils of his Resurrection in the island that you see nearby.'

While he said this he prepared to serve the servants of God and do whatever was necessary for Holy Saturday.

16

When, on Holy Saturday, all was ready and brought to the boat, the man said to Saint Brendan:

'Your boat cannot carry any more. I, therefore, shall bring to you after eight days whatever food and drink you will need until Pentecost.'

Saint Brendan said:

'How do you know where we shall be after eight days?'

He replied:

'Tonight and on Easter Sunday until mid-day you will be in the island that you see nearby. Afterwards you will sail to another island, which is not far from this one towards the west, and which is called the Paradise of Birds. There you will remain until the octave of Pentecost.'

Saint Brendan also questioned him on how the sheep could be so big there as, one could see, they were. They were indeed bigger than cattle. He replied:

'No one takes milk from the sheep in this island, nor does winter put any strain on them. They stay in the pastures always, day and night. As a consequence they are larger here than in the parts you come from.'

They set out for the boat and began to sail, each party having blessed the other.

10 **W**HEN THEY approached the other island, the boat began to ground before they could reach its landing-place. Saint Brendan ordered the brothers to disembark from the boat into the sea, which they did. They held the boat on both sides with ropes until they came to the landing-place. The island was stony and without grass. There were a few pieces of driftwood on it, but no sand on its shore. While the brothers spent the night outside in prayers and vigils, the man of God remained sitting inside in the boat. For he knew the kind of island it was, but he did not want to tell them, lest they be terrified.

When morning came he ordered each of the priests to sing his Mass, which they did. While Saint Brendan was himself singing his Mass in the boat, the brothers began to carry the raw meat out of the boat to preserve it with salt, and also the flesh which they had brought from the other island. When they had done this they put a pot over a fire. When, however, they were plying the fire with wood and the pot began to boil, the island began to be in motion like a wave. The brothers rushed to the boat, crying out for protection to the holy father. He drew each one of them into the boat by his hand. Having left everything they had had on the island behind, they began to sail. Then the island moved out to sea. The lighted fire could be seen over two miles away. Saint Brendan told the brothers what it really was, saying:

'Brothers, are you surprised at what this island has done?'

They said:

'We are very surprised and indeed terror-stricken.'

He said to them:

'My sons, do not be afraid. God revealed to me during the night in a vision the secret of this affair. Where we were was not an island, but a fish — the foremost of all that swim in the ocean. He is always trying to bring his tail to meet his head, but he cannot because of his length. His name is Jasconius.'

THE PARADISE OF BIRDS

𝒲HEN THEY were sailing near the 11 island where they had spent the three days, and came to the western edge of it, they saw another island almost joining it, separated only by a small channel. There was plenty of grass on it; it had groves of trees and was full of flowers. They started circling it, looking for a landing-place. As they were sailing on its southern side they found a stream flowing into the sea and there they put the boat in to land. As they disembarked, Saint Brendan ordered them to draw the boat with ropes up along the river-bed with all their might. The width of the river was about the width of the boat. The father sat in the boat. So they carried on for about a mile, until they came to the source of the stream. Saint Brendan spoke:

'Our Lord Jesus Christ has given us a place in which to stay during his holy Resurrection.'

And he added:

'If we had no other supplies but this spring, it would, I believe, alone be enough for food and drink.'

Over the spring there was a tree of extraordinary girth and no less height covered with white birds. They covered it so much that one could scarcely see its leaves or branches. When the man of God saw this, he began to think and ponder within himself what it meant or what was the reason that such a great multitude of birds could be all collected together. He was so tormented about this that the tears poured out and flowed down upon his cheeks, and he implored God, saying:

'God, who knows the unknown and reveals all that is secret, you know the distress of my heart. I implore your majesty to have pity and reveal to me, a sinner, through your great mercy your secret that I now look upon with my eyes. I rely not on what I deserve or my worth, but rather on your boundless pity.'

When he said this within himself and had taken his seat again, one of the birds flew from the tree, making a noise with her wings like a hand-bell, and took up position on the side of the boat where the man of God was sitting. She sat on the edge of the prow and stretched her wings, as it were as a sign of joy, and looked with a peaceful mien at the holy father. The man of God immediately concluded that God had listened to his plea, and spoke to the bird:

'If you are God's messenger, tell me where these birds come from or for what reason they are congregated here.'

She replied immediately:

'We survive from the great destruction of the ancient enemy, but we were not associated with them through any sin of ours. When we were created, Lucifer's fall and that of his followers brought about our destruction also. But our God is just and true. In his great judgment he sent us here. We endure no sufferings. Here we can see God's presence. But God has separated us from sharing the lot of the others who were faithful. We wander through various regions of the air and the firmament and the earth, just like the other spirits that travel on their missions. But on holy days and Sundays we are given bodies such as you now see so that we may stay here and praise our creator. You and your brothers have now spent one year on your journey. Six still remain. Where you celebrated Easter today, there you will celebrate it every year. Afterwards you will find what you cherish in your heart, that is, the Promised Land of the Saints.'

When she said this, she lifted herself off the prow and flew to the other birds.

When the hour of vespers had come all the birds in the tree chanted, as it were with one voice, beating their wings on their sides:

'A hymn is due to thee, O God, in Zion, and a vow shall be paid to you in Jerusalem.'

They kept repeating this versicle for about the space of an hour. To the man of God and his companions the chant and the sound of their wings seemed in its sweetness like a rhythmical song.

Then Saint Brendan said to his brothers:

'Repair your bodies, for today our souls are filled with divine food.'

When supper was over they performed the divine service. When all was finished, the man of God and his companions gave repose to their bodies until midnight. Waking, the man of God aroused his brothers for the vigil of the holy night, beginning with the versicle:

'Lord, open my lips.'

When the holy man had finished, all the birds responded with wing and mouth, saying:

'Praise the Lord, all his angels; praise him, all his powers.'

So it was as for vespers — they chanted all the time for the space of an hour.

When dawn rose they chanted:

'May the radiance of the Lord, our God, be upon us!' — with the same tune and for the same length of time as at matins and lauds. Likewise at terce they chanted the versicle:

'Sing praises to our God, sing praises! Sing praises to our king. Sing praises in wisdom.'

At sext they chanted:

'Shine your countenance, Lord, upon us, and have mercy on us.'

At nones they chanted:

'How good and pleasant it is that brothers live together as one!'

In this way, day and night, the birds gave praise to the Lord. And so Saint Brendan refreshed his brothers with the feast of Easter until the octave day.

When the days of the octave were over he said:

'Let us take supplies from the spring. Until now we had no need of water except to wash our hands and feet.'

When he said this, the man, with whom they had previously spent the three days before Easter and who had given them food for the feast of Easter, came to them in his boat which was full of food and drink. He took all of this out of the boat, stood before the holy father and said:

'Men, brothers, here you have enough until the holy day of Pentecost. Do not drink from the spring here. It is strong to drink. I shall tell you what kind it is: if a man drinks it, sleep will overpower him and he will not awaken for twenty-four hours. It is only when it is outside of the spring that it has the taste and quality of water.'

When he had received the holy father's blessing, he returned to his own place.

Saint Brendan remained where he was until the beginning of the octave of Pentecost. For the chanting of the birds revived their spirits. On Pentecost, however, when the man of God had sung Mass with

23

his brothers, their steward came, bringing with him whatever was necessary for the celebration of the feast day. When they had sat down together for the meal, the steward spoke to them, saying:

'You have a long journey ahead of you. Take the full of your vessels from the spring here and dry bread which you can keep until next year. I shall give you as much as your boat can carry.'

When all this had been finished, he received the holy father's blessing and returned to his own place.

After eight days Saint Brendan had the boat loaded with all the things the steward had brought to him, and had all the vessels filled from the spring. When all was assembled at the shore, the same bird with speedy flight came and sat on the prow of the boat. The man of God understood that she wanted to tell him something. Then in a human voice she said:

'Next year you will celebrate with us the holy day of Easter and the time you have just spent with us. And where you were this year on Maundy Thursday, there you will be next year on that day. Similarly you will celebrate the vigil of Easter Sunday where you formerly celebrated it, on the back of Jasconius. After eight months you will also find an island which is called the Island of the Community of Ailbe and there you will celebrate Christmas Day.'

When she had said this, she returned to her own place. The brothers stretched the sail and steered out into the ocean, while the birds chanted, as it were with one voice:

'Hear us, God, our saviour, our hope throughout all the boundaries of the earth and in the distant sea.'

THE COMMUNITY OF AILBE

*t*HEN THE holy father, with his group, was driven here and there for three months over the space of the ocean. They could see nothing but sky and sea. They ate always every second or third day.

One day there appeared to them an island not

12

far away. When they were approaching the shore, the wind drew them away from landing. They, therefore, had to circle the island for forty days, and still they could not find a landing-place. The brothers in the boat implored God with tears to give them help. Their strength had almost failed because of their utter exhaustion. When they had persevered for three days in frequent prayer and abstinence, a narrow landing-place appeared to them, just wide enough to take one boat only; and there appeared before them there also two wells, one muddy and the other clear. The brothers then rushed with their vessels to drink the water. The man of God, watching them, said:

'My sons, do not do a forbidden thing, that is, something without permission of the elders who live in this island. They will freely give you the water that you now want to drink in stealth.'

When they disembarked and were wondering in which direction they should go, an elder of great gravity met them. His hair was snow-white and his face was shining. He prostrated himself three times on the ground before embracing the man of God. But Saint Brendan and those with him raised him from the ground. As they embraced one another, the elder held the hand of the holy father and went along with him the distance of about two hundred yards to a monastery. Saint Brendan stood with his brothers before the gate of the monastery and asked the elder:

'Whose monastery is this? Who is in charge of

it? Where do the inhabitants come from?'

The holy father kept questioning the elder in various ways, but he could not get one answer out of him: he only indicated with his hand, with incredible meekness, that they should be silent.

As soon as the holy father realized that this was a rule of the place, he spoke to his brothers, saying:

'Keep your mouths from speaking lest these brothers be defiled by your garrulousness.'

At this remonstrance eleven brothers came to meet them with reliquaries, crosses and hymns, chanting the versicle:

'Rise, saints of God, from your dwellings and go to meet truth. Sanctify the place, bless the people, and graciously keep us your servants in peace.'

When the versicle was finished the father of the monastery embraced Saint Brendan and his companions in order. In the same way his community embraced the companions of the holy man.

When they had exchanged the kiss of peace, they led them to the monastery as the custom is in western parts to conduct brothers in this way with prayers. Afterwards the abbot of the monastery with his monks washed the feet of the guests and chanted the antiphon:

'A new commandment.'

When this was done the abbot led them in great silence to the refectory. A signal was sounded, hands were washed, and then the abbot made them sit down. When a second signal sounded, one of the brothers of the father of the monastery got up and served the table with loaves of extraordinary whiteness and some roots of incredible sweetness. The brothers sat mixed with their guests in order. There was a full loaf between every two brothers. The same server, on the sounding of the signal, gave the brothers drink.

The abbot for his part was urging on the brothers, saying with great glee:

'In joy and fear of the Lord, drink in love now water from the well from which you wanted to drink in stealth today! The feet of the brothers are washed every day from the other, muddy, well that you saw, because it is always warm. We have no idea where the loaves that you see are baked or who carries them to our larder. What we do know is that they are given to his servants from the great charity of God by means of some dependant creature. There are twenty-four of us brothers here. Every day we have twelve loaves for our food, a loaf between every two. On feast-days and Sundays God increases the supply to one full loaf for each brother, so that they can have supper from what is left over. Just now on your coming we have a double supply. Thus Christ feeds us from the time of Saint Patrick and Saint Ailbe, our father, for eighty years until now. Yet neither sign of old age nor weakness spreads in our limbs. On this island we need nothing to eat that is prepared by fire. Neither cold nor heat ever overcomes us. And when the time comes for Masses or vigils, we light in our church the lights that we brought with us from our

28

homeland under divine predestination. They burn till day and still none of them is reduced in any way.'

After they had drunk three times, the abbot sounded a signal in the usual way. The brothers rose all together in great silence and gravity from the table, and preceded the holy fathers to the church. Behind them walked Saint Brendan and the father of the monastery. As they entered the church twelve other brothers, genuflecting quickly, met them on their way out. When Saint Brendan saw them he said:

'Abbot, why did these not eat along with us?'

The father replied:

'Because of you our table could not hold us all together at one sitting. They will now eat and will miss nothing. Let us now, however, go into the church and sing vespers so that our brothers, who are eating now, will be able to sing vespers after us in good time.'

When they had finished the office of vespers Saint Brendan examined how the church was built. It was square, of the same length as breadth, and had seven lights — three before the altar, which was in the middle, and two each before the other two altars. The altars were made of crystal cut in a square, and likewise all the vessels were of crystal, namely patens, chalices and cruets and other vessels required for the divine cult. There were twenty-four seats in a circle in the church. The abbot, however, sat between the two choirs. One group began from

him and ended with him, and it was likewise with
the other. No one on either side presumed to intone
a verse but the abbot. No one in the monastery
spoke or made any sound. If a brother needed anything he went before the abbot, knelt facing him,
and requested within his heart what he needed.
Thereupon the holy father taking a tablet and stylus
wrote as God revealed to him and gave it to the
brother who asked his advice.

While Saint Brendan was reflecting upon all these
matters within himself, the abbot spoke to him :

'Father, it is now time to return to the refectory
so that all that we have to do will be done while
there is light.'

This they did in the same way as before.

When they had completed the day's course in
order, they all hurried with great eagerness to compline. When the abbot had intoned the versicle :

'God, come to my aid,'
and they had together given honour to the Trinity,
they began to chant the versicle :

'We have acted wrongly, we have done iniquity !
You, Lord, who are our faithful father, spare us.
I shall sleep in peace therefore, and shall take my
rest; for you, Lord, have placed me, singularly, in
hope.'

After that they chanted the office of the hour.

When the order of psalms had been completed, all
went out of the church, the brothers bringing their
guests, each to his cell, with them. But the abbot
and Saint Brendan remained seated in the church to

wait for the coming of the light. Saint Brendan questioned the holy father on their silence and their community life: 'how could human flesh endure such a life?'

The father replied with great reverence and humility:

'Abbot, I confess before my Christ. It is eighty years since we came to this island. We have heard no human voice except when singing praise to God. Among the twenty-four of us no voice is raised except by way of a signal given by a finger or the eyes, and that only by the elders. None of us has suffered ill in the flesh or from the spirits that infest the human race, since we came here.'

Saint Brendan said:

'May we stay here now — or not?'

He replied:

'You may not, because it is not the will of God. Why do you ask me, father? Has not God revealed to you, before you came here to us, what you must do? You must return to your own place with fourteen of your brothers. There God has prepared your burial-place. Of the two remaining brothers, one will stay abroad in the Island of the Anchorites, and the other will be condemned by a shameful death to hell.'

While they were thus conversing a fiery arrow sped through a window before their very eyes and lit all the lamps that were placed before the altars. Then the arrow immediately sped out again. But a bright light was left in the lamps. Saint Brendan again asked:

'Who will quench the lights in the morning?'

The holy father replied:

'Come and see the secret of it. You can see the tapers burning in the centre of the bowls. Nothing of them actually burns away so that they might get smaller or reduced in size, nor is there any deposit left in the morning. The light is spiritual.'

Saint Brendan asked:

'How can an incorporeal light burn corporeally in a corporeal creature?'

The elder replied:

'Have you not read of the bush burning at Mount Sinai? Yet that bush was unaffected by the fire.'

They kept vigil the whole night until morning. Then Saint Brendan asked leave to set out on his journey. The elder said to him:

'No, father. You must celebrate Christmas with us until the octave of the Epiphany.'

The holy father, therefore, with his company stayed that time with the twenty-four fathers in the Island of the Community of Ailbe.

THE SOPORIFIC WELL

13 WHEN THE feast-days were over the blessed Brendan and his followers brought provisions into the boat and received the blessing of the holy men. He then sailed out to the ocean as fast as he could. Whether by rowing or sailing, the boat was carried to many different places until the beginning of Lent.

One day they saw an island not far in front of them. When the brothers saw it they began to row eagerly, because they were then very distressed from hunger and thirst. Their food and drink had failed three days before. When the holy father had blessed the landing-place and all had disembarked from the boat, they found a clear well, a variety of plants and roots in a circle around the well, and various kinds of fish swimming along the river-bed into the sea.

Saint Brendan said to his brothers:

'God has given us here a comfort after our toil. Gather the plants and roots which the Lord has prepared for his servants.'

So they did. When they poured out the water to drink it, however, the man of God said to them:

'Brothers, take care that you do not use too much of these waters, lest they lie heavily upon your bodies.'

The brothers interpreted the prescription of the man of God in different ways. Some of them drank one cup, others two, and the rest three. The last were overcome by a sleep of three days and three nights; others by a sleep of two days and two nights; the remainder by a sleep of a day and a night. But the holy father prayed unceasingly to God for his brothers, because through their ignorance such a danger had come upon them.

When the three days' sleeping were up, the holy father spoke to his companions:

'Brothers, let us flee from this threat to our lives

lest something worse happen to us. The Lord gave us sustenance, but you did yourself damage with it. Leave this island, then, taking provisions from the fish, and prepare what you need for a meal every third day up to Maundy Thursday. Likewise for the water — a single cup for each brother each day and equally for the roots.'

When they had loaded the boat with all that the man of God had ordered, they set sail and made out to sea in a northerly direction.

THE COAGULATED SEA

14 AFTER THREE DAYS and three nights the wind dropped and the sea coagulated, as it were — it was so smooth. The holy father said:

'Ship the oars and loosen the sail. Wherever God wants to direct the boat, let him direct it!'

The boat, therefore, was carried around for twenty days. Afterwards God raised a wind favourable to them again, from west to east. They then set sail out to sea and sped on. They ate always every third day.

THE ISLAND OF SHEEP, JASCONIUS AND
THE PARADISE OF BIRDS AGAIN

ONE DAY an island that looked like a cloud **15**
appeared to them a long distance away.
Saint Brendan said:

'My sons, do you recognize that island?'

They said:

'No, not at all.'

He said:

'I recognize it. That is the island where we were last year on Maundy Thursday. That is where our good steward lives.'

The brothers began to row for joy as fast as their strength could support. When the man of God saw this, he said:

'Children, do not tire your limbs foolishly. Is not the all-powerful God the pilot and sailor of our boat? Leave it to him. He himself guides our journey just as he wills.'

When they came near that island, the same steward came to meet them in a boat, and led them to the landing-place where they had disembarked the previous year. He praised God and embraced the feet of every one of them, beginning from the holy father right down to the last, saying:

'God is wonderful in his saints. The God of Israel will himself give valour and strength to his people. Blessed be God.'

When the versicle was over and everything had been taken from the boat, the steward pitched a tent and made ready a bath — for it was Maundy Thursday — and clothed all the brothers with new garments and served them for three days. The brothers for their part celebrated the Passion of the Lord with great attention until Holy Saturday.

When the services for Holy Saturday were completed, spiritual victims sacrificed and supper taken, the steward said to Saint Brendan and those that were with him:

'Go and embark in the boat so that you may celebrate the vigil of the holy Sunday of the Resurrection where you celebrated it last year. And celebrate the Sunday itself until mid-day in the same way. Afterwards, steer for the island which is called the Paradise of Birds, where you were last year from Easter until the octave of Pentecost, and bring with you all the food and drink that are necessary. I shall come to see you on the Sunday after Easter.'

So they did. The steward loaded the boat with loaves and drink and flesh and other good things, as much as it could take. Saint Brendan gave a blessing and embarked. They set sail immediately for the other island.

When they came near the spot where they should disembark from the boat, they saw the pot which they had left behind the year before. Then Saint Brendan disembarking from the boat with his brothers chanted the hymn of the Three Children right to the end. When the hymn was finished, the man of God warned his brothers, saying:

'My sons, watch and pray, that you do not enter into temptation. Reflect on how God has subjected the savage beast under us without any inconvenience to us.'

The brothers, therefore, spent the vigil scattered over the island until matins. From then until about nine o'clock each of the priests offered Mass. Then the blessed Brendan sacrificed the Spotless Lamb to God and said to his brothers:

'Last year I celebrated the Resurrection of the Lord here. I wish to do the same this year.'

They then set out for the island of the birds.

As they came near the landing-place they had chosen on that island, all the birds chanted, as if with one voice, saying:

'Salvation belongs to our God who sits upon the

throne, and to the Lamb!'

And again:

'The Lord God has given us light. Appoint a holy day, with festal branches up to the horn of the altar.'

Thus they chanted and beat their wings for a long time — for about half an hour — until the holy father and his holy companions and the contents of the boat were landed and the holy father had taken his place in his tent.

When he had celebrated there with his community the feasts of Easter, the steward came to them, as he had told them beforehand, on Sunday the octave of Easter, bringing with him all the food needed for human life.

When they sat down to table, the same bird again sat on the prow of the boat, stretching her wings and making a noise like the sound of a great organ. The man of God then realized that she wished to convey a message to him. The bird said:

'God has ordained for you four points of call for four periods of the year until the seven years of your pilgrimage are over, namely, on Maundy Thursday with your steward who is present every year; Easter you will celebrate on the back of the whale; the Easter feasts until the octave of Pentecost with us; Christmas you will celebrate with the Community of Ailbe. Then after seven years and great and varied trials you will find the Promised Land of the Saints that you seek. There you will live for forty days, and afterwards God will bring you back to the land of your birth.'

When the holy father heard this, he prostrated himself on the ground with his brothers, giving thanks and praise to his creator. When the venerable elder had finished this, the bird returned to her own place.

When they had finished eating, the steward said:

'With God's help I shall return to you with your provisions on the feast of the coming of the Holy Spirit upon the Apostles.'

Having received the blessing of the holy father and all that were with him, he returned to his own place. The venerable father remained there the number of days indicated. When the feast days were over, Saint Brendan ordered his brothers to prepare to sail and fill the vessels from the well. They brought the boat to the sea, while the steward came with his own boat laden with food for the brothers. When he had placed all in the boat of the holy man, he embraced all of them and then returned where he had come from.

THE DEVOURING BEAST

tHE VENERABLE FATHER and his com- **16** panions sailed out into the ocean and their boat was carried along for forty days. One day there appeared to them a beast of immense size following them at a distance. He spouted foam from his nostrils and ploughed through the waves at a great speed, as if he were about to devour them. When the brothers saw this they called upon the Lord, saying:

'Deliver us, Lord, so that that beast does not devour us.'

Saint Brendan comforted them, saying:

'Do not be afraid. You have little faith. God, who always defends us, will deliver us from the mouth of this beast and from other dangers.'

As the beast came near them he caused waves of extraordinary height to go before him right up to the boat, so that the brothers were more and more afraid. The venerable elder also raised his hands to heaven and said:

'Lord, deliver your servants, as you delivered David from the hand of Goliath, the giant. Lord, deliver us, as you delivered Jonas from the belly of the whale.'

After these three pleas asking for deliverance, a mighty monster passed near them from the west going to encounter the beast. He immediately attacked him, emitting fire from his mouth. The elder spoke to his brothers:

'Look, my sons, at the great deeds of our Saviour! See how the beasts obey their creator. Wait presently for the outcome of this affair. This battle will do us no damage. It will redound to the glory of God.'

When he had said this the wretched beast that pursued the servants of Christ was cut into three pieces before their eyes. The other returned after his victory to where he had come from.

Another day they saw at a distance a very large island full of trees. While they were drawing near its shore and disembarking from the boat, they saw the end portion of the beast that had been slain. Saint Brendan said:

'See what wished to devour you! You now shall devour it! You will stay a long while in this island. Take your boat, therefore, out of the water high up on the land and look for a place in the wood where your tent can stand.'

The holy father himself determined the spot where they were to stay.

When they had carried out the order of the man of God and had put all the utensils in the tent, Saint Brendan said to his brothers:

'Take your provisions from that beast, enough for three months. For tonight its flesh will be devoured by beasts.'

They were engaged until vespers in carrying up as much flesh from the shore as they required, in accordance with the instruction of the holy father. When the brothers had done all this, they said:

'Abbot, how can we live here without water?'

He answered them:

'Is it more difficult for God to give you water than food? But go to the southern part of the island and you will find a clear well and many plants and roots. Bring me the proper amount of supplies from there.'

They found everything as the man of God had foretold. Saint Brendan, therefore, remained three months, because there was a storm at sea and a strong wind and variable weather with rain and hail.

The brothers went to see what the man of God had said about the beast. When they came to the place where the body was before, they found nothing but bones. They hurried back to the man of God and said:

'Abbot, it is as you said.'

He replied to them:

'I know, my sons, that you wanted to test me, to see if I spoke the truth or not. I shall tell you another sign: a portion of a fish will come there tonight, and tomorrow you will eat of it.'

On the following day, indeed, the brothers went out to the place and they found as the man of God had said. They brought back as much as they could carry. The venerable father said to them:

'Keep it and preserve it carefully with salt. You will have need of it. For God will make the weather fine today, tomorrow and after tomorrow. The swell of the sea and the waves will fall. Then you will leave this place.'

When these days were over Saint Brendan ordered his brothers to load the boat, to fill the containers and other vessels and collect plants and roots for his own use. For the father from the time of his ordination to the priesthood tasted nothing in which the spirit of life drew support from flesh. When all was loaded into the boat, they raised the sail and set off in a northerly direction.

THE ISLAND OF THE THREE CHOIRS
OR ANCHORITES
A LATECOMER STAYS

ONE DAY they saw an island a long distance away from them. Saint Brendan said:
'Do you see that island?'
They replied:
'We do.'
He said to them:
'Three choirs of people are in that island: one of boys, another of youths, a third of elders. And one of your brothers will remain on pilgrimage there.'

The brothers asked him which of them it was. As they were preoccupied with the thought and he saw that they were sad, he said:
'There is the brother who will remain here!'

The brother indicated was one of the three who had followed after Saint Brendan from his monastery. When they were embarking in the boat in their fatherland, he had spoken of their future.

They approached the island until the boat put in at the shore. The island was extraordinarily flat, so much so that it seemed to them to be level with the sea. It had no trees or anything that would move with the wind. It was very spacious and covered with white and purple fruit. There they saw the three choirs, as the man of God had foretold. The space between one choir and another was about the throw of a stone from a sling. They moved continuously here and there, one choir, however, at a time standing in one place and chanting:

'The saints will go from strength to strength and they will see the God of gods in Zion.'

While one choir finished this versicle, another choir stood and began to chant the same song, and this they did without any intermission. The first choir was made up of boys in white garments, the second choir was clothed in blue garments, and the third in purple dalmatics.

It was ten o'clock when they put in at the landing-place on the island. When mid-day came all the choirs began to chant together, singing:

'May God be merciful to us . . .' to the end of the psalm, and 'Be pleased, O God, to deliver me . . .' and likewise the third of the psalms for sext: 'I kept my faith . . .' and the prayer for mercy as above.

Likewise at three o'clock they chanted another three psalms: 'Out of the depths' and 'Behold how good', and 'Praise the Lord, O Jerusalem'.

At vespers they chanted: 'A hymn is due to thee, O God, in Zion', and 'Bless the Lord, O my soul, O Lord my God', and the third of the psalms for vespers: 'Praise the Lord, children'. They then chanted, while seated, the gradual psalms.

When they had finished this chant, a cloud of extraordinary brightness covered the island, but now they could no longer see what they had seen, because of the denseness of the cloud. Nevertheless they continued to hear the voices of those singing their ordinary chant without interruption until matins. Then the choirs began to chant, singing:

44

'Praise the Lord from the heavens', then 'Sing to the Lord', and the third of the psalms of matins: 'Praise the Lord in his saints'. After that they chanted twelve psalms in the order of the Psalter.

When day dawned the island was cloudless, and immediately they chanted the three psalms: 'Have mercy on me, O God', 'God, my God, from the dawn I keep watch for thee', and 'Lord, my refuge'.

At terce they chanted another three psalms, that is: 'All peoples', and 'God, in your name', and the third: 'I have loved, because' with the Alleluia.

They then offered up the Spotless Lamb and all came to communion, saying:

'Take this holy body of the Lord and blood of the Saviour for everlasting life.'

When the sacrifice was over, two members of the choir of youths carried a basket full of purple fruit and placed it in the boat, saying:

'Accept fruit from the Island of Strong Men, give us our brother, and set forth in peace.'

Then Saint Brendan called the brother to him and said:

'Embrace your brothers and go with those who summon you. It was a good hour that your mother conceived you, seeing that you have deserved to live with such a community.'

When he had embraced all, including the holy father, Saint Brendan said to him:

'Son, remember the great favours God conferred on you in this life. Go, and pray for us.'

He immediately followed the two youths to their school.

The venerable father and his companions set sail. When it was three o'clock, he ordered his brothers to refresh their bodies with the fruit of the Island of Strong Men. As he said this the man of God took one of them. When he saw its size and that it was full of juice, he expressed wonder and said:

'I have never seen or gathered fruit of such size.'

They were all of equal size and like a large ball. The man of God then asked that a vessel be brought to him. He squeezed one of the fruits and got a pound of juice from it, which he divided into twelve ounces. The holy father gave an ounce of the juice to each of the brothers. One fruit, therefore, fed one brother for twelve days so that he always had in his mouth the taste of honey.

THE ISLAND OF GRAPES

18 AFTER SOME DAYS the holy father prescribed a fast for three days. Then when the three days were over a great bird was seen flying near the boat, carrying a branch of an unknown tree. At the tip of the branch was a cluster of grapes of extraordinary redness. The bird dropped this cluster from its beak into the saint's lap. Then Saint Brendan called the attention of his brothers and said:

'Look at the meal that God has sent you. Take it.'

The grapes of this cluster were as big as apples. The man of God divided them, one each among his brothers, and so they had food until the twelfth day.

Again the man of God renewed with his brothers the same fast for three days. Now on the third day they saw an island not far from them, covered completely with densely planted trees bearing the same crop of grapes of such incredible fertility that all the trees were bent down to the ground, with the same fruit of the same colour. No tree was barren, nor was there a tree of any other kind in that island. The brothers then put into harbour. The man of God disembarked and began to walk round the island. It had a perfume like that of a house filled with pomegranates. Meanwhile the brothers were waiting in the boat until the man of God should return to them. All the while the breeze bore in on them a sweet perfume, so that they were tempted to be heedless of their fasts. The venerable father found six copious wells full of flourishing plants and roots of many kinds. He then returned to his brothers, carrying with him some of the first fruits of the island and said to them:

'Disembark, pitch your tent and refresh yourselves with the good fruits of this land that the Lord has shown us.'

And so for forty days they fed on the grapes and on the plants and roots of the wells. But at the end of that time they embarked, bringing with them as much of the fruits as their boat could carry.

THE GRYPHON

19 *W*HEN THEY had gone on board, the boat's sail was hoisted to steer where the wind directed. After they had sailed, the bird called the Gryphon appeared to them, flying from far away towards them. When his brothers saw it they started saying to the holy father:

'That beast has come to devour us.'

The man of God said to them:

'Do not be afraid. God is our helper. He will defend us on this occasion too.'

The bird stretched her talons to seize the servants of God. Just then, suddenly, the bird which on the earlier occasion brought them the branch with the fruits, flew swiftly up to the Gryphon, which immediately made to devour her. But that bird defended herself until she overcame and tore out the eyes of the Gryphon. The Gryphon then flew high up into the sky so that the brothers could scarcely see her. But her killer pursued her until she killed her. For the Gryphon's body fell into the sea near the boat before the eyes of the brothers. The other bird returned to her own place.

THE COMMUNITY OF AILBE AGAIN

20 *N*OT MANY DAYS afterwards, Saint Brendan and his sailors caught sight of the Island of the Community of Ailbe. There he celebrated Christmas with his brothers. When the feast-days were over, the venerable father received the

blessing of the abbot and his community and then sailed round the ocean for a long time — except for the feasts mentioned, that is Easter and Christmas. For during them he rested in the places mentioned.

THE CLEAR SEA

IT HAPPENED on one occasion that as Brendan **21** was celebrating the feast of Saint Peter the Apostle in his boat, they found the sea so clear that they could see whatever was underneath them. When they looked into the deep they saw the different kinds of fish lying on the sand below. It even seemed to them that they could touch them with their hands, so clear was that sea. They were like herds lying in pastures. They were so numerous that they looked like a city of circles as they lay, their heads touching their tails.

His brothers asked the venerable father to celebrate his Mass in silence, lest the fish would hear and come up to pursue them. The holy father smiled and said to them:

'I am surprised at your foolishness. Why are you afraid of those fish when you were not afraid of the devourer and master of all the fish of the sea, sitting and singing psalms, as you often did, on his back? Indeed you cut wood and lit a fire and cooked meat there! Why then are you afraid of those? Is not our Lord Jesus Christ God of all fish, and can he not reduce all living things?'

When he said these things he began to intone as loudly as he could. Others of the brothers kept their eyes on the fish all the time. When the fish heard him singing, they came up from the bottom and began to swim in a circle round the boat — in such a way that the brothers could not see beyond the fish anywhere, so great was the multitude of the different fishes swimming. Still they did not come near the boat, but kept swimming at a distance in a wide arc. And so they kept swimming here and there until the man of God finished Mass. After this, as if they were taking flight, they all swam by different paths of the ocean away from the sight of the servants of God. It took eight days for Saint Brendan, even with a favouring wind and all his canvas stretched to the full, to cross the clear sea.

THE CRYSTAL PILLAR

22 ONE DAY when they had celebrated their Masses, a pillar in the sea appeared to them that seemed to be not far distant. Still it took them three days to come up to it. When the man of God approached it he tried to see the top of it — but he could not, it was so high. It was higher than the sky. Moreover a wide-meshed net was wrapped around it. The mesh was so wide that the boat could pass through its openings. They could not decide of what substance the net was made. It had the colour of silver, but they thought that it seemed harder than marble. The pillar was of bright crystal.

Brendan spoke to his brothers:

'Ship the oars and take down the mast and sail. Let some of you at the same time take hold of the meshes of the net.'

There was a large space, roughly about a mile, at all points between the net and the pillar, and likewise the net went down a similar distance into the sea. When they had done what they had been ordered, the man of God said to them:

'Let the boat in through one of the meshes, so that we can have a close look at the wonders of our creator.'

When they had gone in and looked around here and there, the sea was as clear to them as glass, so that they could see everything that was underneath. They could examine the foundations of the pillar and also the edge of the net lying on the sea bed. The light of the sun was as bright below as above the water.

Then Saint Brendan measured the four sides of the opening of the net: it was about six to seven feet on every side.

They then sailed throughout the whole day near one side of the pillar and in its shadow they could still feel the heat of the sun. They stayed there until three o'clock. The man of God kept measuring the one side. The measurement of each of the four sides of that pillar was the same, namely about seven hundred yards. The venerable father was engaged for four days in this way around the four angles of the pillar.

On the fourth day, however, they found a chalice, of the same substance as the net, and a paten, of the same colour as the pillar, lying in a window in the side of the pillar facing the south. Saint Brendan took hold of these vessels immediately, saying:

'Our Lord Jesus Christ has shown us this wonder, and given me these two gifts, so that the wonder be manifested to many in order that they may believe.'

Then the man of God ordered his brothers to perform the divine office and then refresh their bodies, for they had had no slack time in which to take food or drink since they had seen the pillar.

When the night was over the brothers began to row towards the north. When they had passed through an opening in the net they raised the mast and sail, while some of the brothers still held the meshes of the net until all was made ready on the boat. When the sail had been spread, a favouring wind began to blow behind them so that they did not need to row but only to hold the ropes and rudder. So their boat was borne along for eight days towards the north.

THE ISLAND OF SMITHS

23 AFTER EIGHT DAYS they caught sight of an island not far away, very rough, rocky and full of slag, without trees or grass, full of

smiths' forges. The venerable father said to his brothers:

'I am troubled about this island. I do not want to go on it or even come near it. But the wind is bringing us directly there.'

As they were sailing for a moment beside it, a stone's throw away, they heard the sound of bellows blowing, as if it were thunder, and the blows of hammers on iron and anvils. When he heard this the venerable father armed himself, making the sign of the Lord in all four directions, saying:

'Lord, Jesus Christ, deliver us from this island.'

When the man of God had finished speaking, one of the inhabitants of the island was seen to come out of doors apparently to do something or other. He was very shaggy and full at once of fire and darkness. When he saw the servants of Christ pass near the island, he went back into his forge. The man of God blessed himself again and said to his brothers:

'My sons, raise the sail higher still and row as fast as you can and let us flee from this island.'

Even before he had finished speaking, the same savage came to the shore near where they were, carrying a tongs in his hands that held a lump of burning slag of immense size and heat. He immediately threw the lump on top of the servants of Christ, but it did no hurt to them. It passed more than two hundred yards above them. Then the sea, where it fell, began to boil, as if a volcano were erupting there. The smoke rose from the sea as from a fiery furnace.

But when the man of God had got about a mile away from the spot where the lump fell, all the islanders came to the shore, each of them carrying a lump of his own. Some of them began to throw the lumps after the servants of Christ into the sea, the one throwing his lump over the other, all the while going back to the forges and setting the lumps on fire. It looked as if the whole island was ablaze, like one big furnace, and the sea boiled, just as a cooking pot full of meat boils when it is well plied with fire. All day long they could hear a great howling from the island. Even when they could no longer see it, the howling of its denizens still reached their ears, and the stench of the fire assailed their nostrils. The holy father comforted his monks, saying:

'Soldiers of Christ, be strengthened in faith unfeigned and in spiritual weapons, for we are in the confines of Hell. So, be on the watch and be brave.'

THE FIERY MOUNTAIN
THE THIRD LATECOMER TAKEN
BY DEMONS

24 ON ANOTHER DAY there appeared to them, as it were through the clouds, a high mountain in the ocean, not far away towards the north. It was very smoky on top. Immediately the wind drew them very fast to the shore of that island until the boat stopped a little distance from the land.

The cliff was so high that they could scarcely see the top of it. It was also the colour of coal and unusually perpendicular, just like a wall.

The one remaining of the three brothers, who followed after Saint Brendan from his monastery, jumped out of the boat and began to walk up to the base of the cliff. Then he cried out:

'Alas for me, father, I am being snatched from you and am powerless to come back to you.'

The brothers straightaway began to turn the boat from the land and call on the Lord, saying:

'Have mercy on us, Lord, have mercy on us.'

The venerable father and his companions saw how the unhappy man was carried off by a multitude of demons to be tormented and was set on fire among them. He said:

'Alas for you, my son, that you have received such fate as you have deserved while living.'

Again a favouring wind brought them towards the south. When they looked back for a distance at the island, they saw that the mountain was no longer covered with smoke, but was spouting flames from itself up to the ether and then breathing back, as it were, the same flames again upon itself. The whole mountain from the summit right down to the sea looked like one big pyre.

25 **W**HEN SAINT BRENDAN had sailed towards the south for seven days, there appeared to them in the sea the outline as it were of a man sitting on a rock with a cloth suspended between two small iron fork-shaped supports about a cloak's length in front of him. The object was being tossed about by the waves just like a little boat in a whirlwind. Some of the brothers said that it was a bird, others a boat. When the man of God heard them discussing the matter among themselves, he said:

'Cease arguing. Steer the boat to the spot.'

When the man of God drew near, the waves, glued as it were in a circle, kept them at a distance. They found a man, shaggy and unsightly, sitting on a rock. As the waves flowed towards him from every side, they struck him even to the top of his head. When they receded, the bare rock where the unhappy man was sitting was exposed. The wind also sometimes drove the cloth hanging in front of him away from him, and sometimes blew it against his eyes and forehead.

Blessed Brendan questioned him as to who he was, or for what fault he was sent here, or what he deserved to justify the imposition of such penance? The man replied:

'I am unhappy Judas, the most evil trader ever. I am not here in accordance with my deserts but because of the ineffable mercy of Jesus Christ. This

place is not reckoned as punishment but as an indulgence of the Saviour in honour of the Lord's Resurrection.'

That day was in fact the Lord's day.

'When I am sitting here I feel as if I were in a paradise of delights in contrast with my fear of the torments that lie before me this evening. For I burn, like a lump of molten lead in a pot, day and night, in the centre of the mountain that you have seen. Leviathan and his attendants are there. I was there when he swallowed your brother. Hell was so joy-ful that it sent forth mighty flames — as it always does when it devours the souls of the impious. But here I have a place of refreshment every Sunday from evening to evening, at Christmas until the

Epiphany, at Easter until Pentecost, and on the feasts of the purification and assumption of the Mother of God. After and before these feasts I am tortured in the depth of Hell with Herod and Pilate and Annas and Caiphas. And so I beseech you through the Saviour of the world to be good enough to intercede with the Lord Jesus Christ that I be allowed to remain here until sunrise tomorrow, so that the demons may not torture me on your coming and bring me to the fate I have purchased with such an evil bargain.'

Saint Brendan said to him :

'May the Lord's will be done! Tonight until the morning you will not be eaten by the demons.'

The man of God questioned him again, saying :

'What is the meaning of this cloth?'

The other replied :

'I gave this cloth to a leper when I was procurator for the Lord. But it was not mine to give. It belonged to the Lord and the brothers. And so it gives me no relief but rather does me hurt. Likewise the iron forks, on which it hangs, I gave to the priests of the temple to hold up cooking-pots. With the rock on which I sit I filled a trench in the public road to support the feet of those passing by, before I was a disciple of the Lord.'

When the evening hour had darkened the sea, an innumerable number of demons covered its surface in a circle, shouting and saying :

'Go away, man of God, from us. We cannot come near our companion until you go away from him.

Neither have we dared to look on the face of our chief until we return his friend to him. You have taken our mouthful away from us. Do not protect him this night.'

The man of God said to them:

'I do not protect him, but the Lord Jesus Christ allowed him to remain here this night until morning.'

The demons retorted:

'How can you invoke the Lord's name over him, when he is himself the betrayer of the Lord?'

The man of God said to them:

'I order you in the name of our Lord Jesus Christ that you do him no evil until morning.'

When, therefore, that night was passed, and when the man of God had begun to set out on his journey, an infinite number of demons was seen to cover the face of the ocean, emitting dire sounds and saying:

'Man of God, we curse your coming as well as your going, since our chief whipped us last night with terrible scourges because we did not bring to him that accursed prisoner.'

The man of God said to them:

'Your curse does not affect us, but rather yourselves. The man whom you curse is blessed; he whom you bless is cursed.'

The demons answered him:

'Unhappy Judas will suffer double punishment for the next six days because you protected him in the night that has passed.'

The venerable father said to them:

59

'You have no power over that, nor your chief:
God will have the power.'

And he added:

'I order you and your chief in the name of our
Lord Jesus Christ not to inflict on him more torments than before.'

They answered him:

'Are you the Lord of all, so that we obey your
words?'

The man of God said to them:

'I am his servant, and whatever I order, I order
in his name. My service lies in those matters which
he has assigned to me.'

The demons followed him until Judas could no
longer be seen. They then returned and lifted up the
unhappy soul among them with great force and
howling.

THE ISLAND OF PAUL THE HERMIT

26 BUT SAINT BRENDAN and his comrades
sailed towards the south, glorifying God in
all. On the third day there appeared to them a small
island far away to the south. When his brothers had
begun to row faster and they had come near the
island, Saint Brendan said to them:

'Men, brothers, do not tire your bodies overmuch.
You have enough toil. It is seven years to the
coming Easter since we left our fatherland. You

will now see Paul the spiritual Hermit, who has
lived in this island for sixty years without any
bodily food. For the previous thirty years he got
food from an animal.'

When they had got to the shore they could not
find a landing-place because of the height of the
cliff. The island was small and circular — about
two hundred yards in circumference. There was
no earth on it, but it looked a naked rock like
flint. It was as long as it was broad and as it was
high. When they had rowed around the island they
discovered a landing-place so narrow that it could
scarcely take the prow of the boat and disembar-
kation was very difficult. Saint Brendan then said to
his brothers:

'Wait here until I return to you. You may not go on land without permission from the man of God who lives in this spot.'

When the venerable father had come to the top of the island, he saw two caves, the entrance of one facing the entrance of the other, on the side of the island facing east. He also saw a minuscule spring, round like a plate, flowing from the rock before the entrance to the cave where the soldier of Christ lived. When the spring overflowed, the rock immediately absorbed the water. When Saint Brendan had come near the door of one of the caves, the elder came out to meet him from the other, saying:

'How good and joyful it is that brothers live together.'

When he said this he requested Saint Brendan to order all the brothers to come from the boat. As they embraced him and sat down he called each of them by his own name. When the brothers heard this, they greatly wondered not only at his power of divining, but also at his dress. For he was entirely covered by his hair from his head and beard and other hair down to his feet, and all the hair was white as snow on account of his great age. They could see only his face and eyes. He had no other clothing on him except the hair that grew from his body. When Saint Brendan saw this he was discouraged within himself and said:

'Alas for me who wear a monk's habit and have many owing allegiance to me by virtue of being monks: Here I see sitting before me a man already

62

in the angelic state, untouched by the vices of the body, although he is still in human flesh.'

The man of God said to him:

'Venerable father, how great and marvellous are the wonders that God has shown you that he did not show to any of the holy fathers! You say in your heart that you are not worthy to carry the habit of a monk. But you are greater than a monk! A monk uses the labour of his hands with which to clothe himself. But God from his own secret supplies feeds and clothes both you and your companions for seven years. And I, unhappy, sit here like a bird on this rock, naked but for my hair.'

Saint Brendan then questioned him on his coming and where he came from and for how long he had endured such a life there. The other answered him.

'I was brought up in the monastery of Saint Patrick for fifty years where I looked after the cemetery of the brothers. One day, when my director had pointed out to me the place to bury one who had died, an unknown elder appeared to me and said: "Do not make a grave there, brother, for it is the burial place of another." I said to him: "Father, who are you?" He said: "Why do you not recognize me? Am I not your abbot?" I said to him: "Saint Patrick, my abbot?" He replied: "I am he. I died yesterday. That is the place of my burial. Make the grave of our brother here and tell no one what I have told you. But go tomorrow to the sea shore. There you will find a boat. Embark in it and it will bring you to the spot where you will await the day of your death."

'In the morning I went, in accordance with the holy father's command, to the shore and found exactly what he had told me I would find. When I had embarked, I sailed for three days and three nights. After that I let the boat go wherever the wind would drive it. Then on the seventh day this rock appeared to me. I got on to it immediately, letting the boat go and kicking it with my foot so that it would go back to where it came from. Straightaway I saw it ploughing waves like furrows through the plains of the sea so as to return to its home. But I stayed here. About three o'clock in the afternoon an otter brought me a meal from the sea, that is, one fish in his mouth. He also brought a small bundle of firewood to make a fire, carrying it between his front paws while walking on his two hind legs. When he had put the fish and kindling in front of me he returned where he came from. I took iron, struck flint, made a fire from the kindling and made a meal for myself on the fish. Thus it was for thirty years — always every third day the same servant brought the same food, that is one fish, to do for three days. I ate a third of the fish each day. By God's grace I had no thirst — but on Sunday a trickle of water came forth from the rock, and from this I could drink and fill my little container with water to wash my hands. Then after thirty years I found these two caves and this well. On it I live. For sixty years since, I have lived on this well without nourishment of any other food. I have been ninety years on this island, living on fish for thirty years and on the food afforded by the well for sixty. I lived for fifty years in my native land. The sum of the years of my life until now is one hundred and forty. Here I have but to await in the flesh, as I have been assured, the day of my judgment. Go then to your native land, and bring with you vessels filled with water from this well. You must do this since you have a journey before you of forty days, which will take you till Holy Saturday. You will celebrate Holy Saturday and Easter Sunday and the holy days of Easter where you have celebrated them for the last six years. You will then, having received the blessing of your steward, set out for the Promised Land of the Saints. There you will stay for forty days and then the God of your fathers will bring you safe and sound to the land of your birth.'

THE ISLAND OF SHEEP, JASCONIUS AND THE PARADISE OF BIRDS AGAIN

27

SAINT BRENDAN, therefore, and his brothers, having received the blessing of the man of God, began to sail towards the south for the whole of Lent. Their boat was carried hither and thither, and their only food was the water which they had got on the island of the man of God. This they took every third day and, remaining untouched by hunger or thirst, all were joyful.

Then, as the man of God had foretold, they came to the island of the steward on Holy Saturday. As they arrived at the landing-place he came to meet them with great joy, and helped each of them out of the boat on his arm. When they had finished the divine office for the holy day, he spread supper before them. When evening came they embarked in their boat and the steward came with them.

When they had set sail they found the fish immediately in his usual place. There they sang praise to God all night and Masses in the morning. When Mass was over, however, Jasconius began to go his own way, and all the brothers who were with Saint Brendan began to call on the Lord, saying:

'Hear us, God, our Saviour, our hope throughout all the boundaries of the earth and in the distant sea.'

Saint Brendan comforted his brothers, saying:

'Do not be afraid. You will suffer no evil. Help for the journey is upon us.'

The fish went in a straight course to the shore of the island of the birds. There they stayed until the octave of Pentecost.

When the season of feast-days was over, the steward, who was with them, said to Saint Brendan:

'Embark in your boat and fill your water vessels from this well. This time I shall be the companion and guide of your journey. Without me you will not be able to find the Promised Land of the Saints.'

As they embarked in the boat, all the birds that were on the island began to say as it were with one voice:

'May God, the salvation of all of us, prosper your journey.'

THE PROMISED LAND OF THE SAINTS

SAINT BRENDAN and those who were with **28**
him sailed to the island of the steward, who was with them, and there they took on board provision for forty days. Their voyage was for forty days towards the east. The steward went to the front of the boat and showed them the way. When the forty days were up, as the evening drew on, a great fog enveloped them, so that one of them could hardly see another. The steward, however, said to Saint Brendan :

'Do you know what fog that is ?'

Saint Brendan replied :

'What ?'

Then the other said :

'That fog encircles the island for which you have been searching for seven years.'

After the space of an hour a mighty light shone all around them again and the boat rested on the shore.

On disembarking from the boat they saw a wide land full of trees bearing fruit as in autumn time. When they had gone in a circle around that land, night had still not come on them. They took what fruit they wanted and drank from the wells and so for the space of forty days they reconnoitred the

whole land and could not find the end of it. But one day they came upon a great river flowing through the middle of the island. Then Saint Brendan said to his brothers:

'We cannot cross this river and we do not know the size of this land.'

They had been considering these thoughts within themselves when a youth met them and embraced them with great joy and, calling each by his name, said:

'Happy are they that live in your house. They shall praise you from generation to generation.'

When he said this, he spoke to Saint Brendan:

'There before you lies the land which you have sought for a long time. You could not find it immediately because God wanted to show you his varied secrets in the great ocean. Return, then, to the land of your birth, bringing with you some of the fruit of this land and as many of the precious stones as your boat can carry. The final day of your pilgrimage draws near so that you may sleep with your fathers. After the passage of many times this land will become known to your successors, when persecution of the Christians shall have come. The river that you see divides the island. Just as this land appears to you ripe with fruit, so shall it remain always without any shadow of night. For its light is Christ.'

Saint Brendan with his brothers, having taken samples of the fruits of the land and of all its varieties of precious stones, took his leave of the blessed steward and the youth. He then embarked in his boat and began to sail through the middle of the fog. When they had passed through it, they came to the island called the Island of Delights. They availed themselves of three days' hospitality there and then, receiving a blessing, Saint Brendan returned home directly.

RETURN HOME AND DEATH OF SAINT BRENDAN

tHE BROTHERS received him with thanksgiving, glorifying God who was unwilling that they should be deprived of seeing so lovable a   **29**

father by whose absence they were for so long orphaned. Then the blessed man, commending them for their love, told them everything that he remembered happening on his journey and the great and marvellous wonders God deigned to show him.

Finally he mentioned also the speed of his approaching death — emphasizing its certainty — according to the prophecy of the youth in the Promised Land of the Saints. The outcome proved this to be correct. For when he had made all arrangements for after his death, and a short time had intervened, fortified by the divine sacraments, he migrated from among the hands of his disciples in glory to the Lord, to whom is honour and glory from generation to generation. Amen. End.